The Trucking Bible For Women

Your No-Fluff Guide to Building an Empire on Wheels

BB

BOOKED &
BRANDED
PUBLISHING

STEPHANIE WILLIAMS, MBA

COPYRIGHT

DISCLAIMER

This book is for educational and informational purposes only. It is not legal, tax, or compliance advice. Please confirm all requirements (licensing, permits, insurance, tax structure, etc.)with your local authorities, state agencies, or a qualified professional. Regulations change often, and your situation is unique.

The insights shared are based on the author's personal experience and research at the time of publication. This content was developed independently and does not represent the views or positions of Verizon, Verizon Connect, or any affiliated entity. Use this guide to get informed and take confident action — but always protect your business with proper due diligence.

You're the CEO now. Own it.

Booked & Branded Publishing

DEDICATION

To every woman who's ever said,

"I want more — I just don't know where to start."

This is for you.

To the Black and Brown women building legacies with no blueprint...

To the ones starting over, starting from scratch, or starting scared...

To the woman ready to make her next move her best move...

This book is your permission to go all in.

Welcome to your empire — on wheels.

TABLE OF CONTENTS

INTRODUCTION

Build the Business. Keep the Freedom.

If you picked up this book, you're already thinking differently.

You don't just want a paycheck — you want ownership.

Maybe you're sick of punching a clock.

Maybe you're tired of hearing "trucking is where the money's at" — and wondering how to get in without getting scammed or overwhelmed.

Or maybe you've already dipped your toe in and now you're ready to go all in — but you need guidance you can actually trust.

This book? It's for all of that.

What You'll Get Inside

This is a no-fluff, beginner-friendly guide to building your own trucking business!

— whether you want to drive, dispatch, own a fleet, or work behind the scenes.

- You don't need to come from the industry.

- You don't need $50K in cash to get started.

- You don't need a CDL.

You just need **real strategy** — and someone who's not here to sell you a course or overcomplicate the game.

Who This Book Is For?

Women ready to step into ownership

Anyone who wants to build wealth in a male-dominated space — and stay in control of the business

Aspiring dispatchers, fleet owners, or logistics bosses

Women of color who want a seat at the table **and equity

Booked & Branded Publishing

CHAPTER 1

So You Wanna Start a Trucking Business?

Let's talk.

If you picked up this book, chances are you're hungry for something more. Maybe you're tired of clocking in. Maybe you want freedom. Maybe you've been watching YouTube videos and side-eyeing your paycheck, wondering why everybody else seems to be getting money in trucking but you're still stuck at square one.

If that's you? You're in the right place.

Let's get one thing straight from the jump:

Trucking is not just about driving. It's about ownership.

It's about positioning yourself in an industry that never sleeps —one that feeds families, keeps shelves stocked, moves billion-dollar economies — and claiming your piece of it.

Why Trucking?

Because trucking doesn't care where you went to school, who you know, or what you look like. If you show up with a business mindset and a willingness to learn the game, there is

where hustle meets strategy

room for you at the table — or better yet, you can build your own.

We're talking about a 900+ billion-dollar industry that literally

keeps the country running. If the trucks stop, the country stops. That means opportunity isn't going anywhere.

What you're really stepping into here is power — but it comes with responsibility.

This book? It's your playbook.

What You're Gonna Learn?

This isn't another hype book that makes trucking sound like easy money. I'm not here to sell you a dream — I'm here to hand you the steps.

You'll learn:

- What business structure to choose and how to set it up legally

- The difference between being a driver and being the boss

- How to get your authority and stay compliant

- What kind of insurance you need and what it actually costs

- How to buy or lease a truck — the smart way

- How dispatching and brokering really work

Booked & Branded Publishing

- How to start with one truck or no truck

- How to grow your company without losing your mind

- Whether you're starting from zero, pivoting from a 9–5, or trying to make trucking make sense — this is for you.

If You Only Take One Thing From This Chapter

Let it be this:

- You do not need to have it all figured out before you start.

- You just need the right information, the right mindset, and the confidence to move.

- Let's build something powerful.

- Let's build it with intention.

- Let's build your empire — on wheels.

CHAPTER 2

CDL vs No CDL — What You Really Need to Get Started

Let's clear this up early: you do not need a CDL to own a trucking company.

Can a CDL help? Sure.

Is it required? Nope.

But the key is knowing how you want to position yourself in the business.

So, ask yourself:

- Do I want to drive the truck myself?

- Or do I want to be the owner, running operations, building contracts, and hiring licensed drivers?

If your goal is freedom, scaling, and long-term income without always being on the road — you're probably leaning toward the second option.

What Is a CDL?

A CDL is a Commercial Driver's License, required to legally operate large or specialized commercial vehicles — like semis, buses, or hazardous materials trucks.

where hustle meets strategy

There are three main types:

- Class A: Tractor-trailers, flatbeds, tankers — this is the big one.

- Class B: Straight trucks, dump trucks, box trucks.

- Class C: Passenger vans and smaller HAZMAT transport.

But here's the key:

You can own a company, buy a truck, get your authority, and make money — without ever driving.

You just need someone else with a CDL to operate the vehicle legally if the load requires it.

Booked & Branded Publishing

CDL vs No CDL: Pros and Cons

Without CDL	
Pros	**Cons**
Direct control over your loads	CDL school can cost $3K–$7K
Ability to drive in emergencies	Requires time and physical effort
Save money by driving yourself at startup	"Greater responsibility for safety compliance while driving"
Can step in if a driver quits unexpectedly	"Potential burnout from driving and managing operations"
Flexibility to handle short-notice loads	"Time spent on the road may limit networking or business growth."

Without CDL	
Pros	**Cons**
More time to focus on business growth	
Can hire experienced drivers	
Easier to step into an ownership-only role	Must rely on others to operate trucks
No backup plan if a driver quits	
May require more upfront capital for hiring	

Booked & Branded Publishing

Real Talk:

Many women I work with choose the no-CDL route and build from there. They hire licensed drivers, lease on to carriers, or even launch dispatch businesses while stacking capital to expand. If you're focused, coachable, and ready to treat this like a real business — you can win in trucking without touching a steering wheel.

Let's keep going.

CHAPTER 3

Setting Up the Business Side

Now that you've decided how you want to enter trucking, let's make it real. That means treating your business like... well... a business. Before you grab the keys, you need to handle the paper.

Step 1: Choose Your Legal Business Structure

Most trucking companies go with:

LLC (Limited Liability Company) — most popular for protection and flexibility

Sole Proprietor — fastest and cheapest, but no separation between you and the business

Corporation (S-Corp or C-Corp) — less common at the beginning unless you're building big with investors

Pro Tip: Go with an LLC if you're unsure. You can always change it later. It protects your personal assets and keeps your business legit from the start.

Step 2: Register Your Business

Once you choose your structure:

- File your Articles of Organization (usually through your state's Secretary of State website)

- Pay your registration fee (ranges $50–$300 depending on the state)

- Choose a Registered Agent — this can be you, but many prefer using a service

Step 3: Get Your EIN

Think of your EIN (Employer Identification Number) as your business's Social Security number.

You'll need it to:

- Open a business bank account

- Apply for loans or lines of credit

- Hire employees or contractors

- You can apply free at irs.gov.

Step 4: Open a Business Bank Account

Keep your business and personal money separate. Trust me, you'll thank yourself during tax time — and it also makes your company look more professional to lenders, insurers, and future partners.

Step 5: Get a Business Address, Email, and Phone Number

Even if you're running everything from your kitchen table right now, set yourself up like a business from the beginning:

- Use a virtual business address (like iPostal1 or Anytime Mailbox)
- Set up a professional email (like dispatch@yourcompany.com)
- Get a business phone line (try Google Voice or a VoIP service like Grasshopper)

These things make a difference when you're applying for loans, MC numbers, or working with brokers. They're looking for legit companies — not side hustles.

Real Talk: You don't have to be perfect — just professional.

Set the foundation strong now so when the money comes in, you're ready to scale.

CHAPTER 4

Getting Your Authority & Staying Compliant

If you're starting your own trucking company, getting your authority is one of the most important steps in going legit. "Authority" basically means you have the legal right to operate as a for-hire carrier — and you'll need to get approved at both the state and federal levels. If that sounds like a lot, don't panic — we're breaking it all the way down.

Do You Need Authority?

If you're hauling someone else's freight across state lines and getting paid for it, the answer is almost always yes. Even if you're running under someone else's authority temporarily (which we'll explain more in a bit), eventually you'll want your own so you can maximize your profits and control.

Step 1: Get a USDOT Number

This number identifies your company and tracks your safety history, inspections, and crash reports.

where hustle meets strategy

- Go to the FMCSA Unified Registration System (URS):

- https://www.fmcsa.dot.gov/registration

- Choose New Company Registration.

- You'll need to know your business structure, your EIN (or SSN), and the types of cargo you plan to haul.

- If you're not sure what to pick for everything, the FMCSA provides guidance during the application.

Once approved, your USDOT number will be issued immediately.

Step 2: Apply for an MC Number

Your MC (Motor Carrier) number is what gives you the legal right to transport goods for hire across state lines. Without it, you're basically grounded.

- You apply for this through the same FMCSA site (after you get your USDOT).

- There is a $300 filing fee.

- Once submitted, there's a 21-day public vetting period before your authority becomes active.

Step 3: File a BOC-3 (Designation of Process Agent)

This part gets skipped a lot — but it's required.

- The BOC-3 assigns a legal agent in every state where you do business, in case you're ever sued or need to be served.

- Most people hire a BOC-3 filing service, which costs about $25–$50.

- Once filed, it becomes part of your public record with FMCSA.

Step 4: Get Insurance Lined Up (Don't Skip This)

Pro Tip: Many filing services will also help you monitor compliance deadlines.

You'll need to show proof of liability insurance before your authority becomes active.

- FMCSA requires at least $750,000 in liability coverage (though $1 million is more common and often required by brokers).

- Your insurance company must file a Form BMC-91 or BMC-91X directly with the FMCSA.

Wait to pay for the policy until you have your MC number — but line up quotes ahead of time so you're not delayed.

What About Amazon Relay?

If you're interested in running for Amazon Relay, you'll still need your own active authority to qualify. They require:

- Active DOT and MC numbers

- A minimum of $1 million in auto liability and $100K in cargo insurance

- A carrier score above a certain threshold

So even if your goal is to contract with Amazon rather than find your own loads, getting your authority is still step one.

CHAPTER 5

Buying, Renting, or Leasing a Truck

Now that your paperwork's handled, let's talk about the truck itself — aka your mobile money-maker. Whether you're buying it outright or leasing it from someone else, you need to make the best financial decision for your goals and budget.

Option 1: Buying Your Truck

Pros:

- You own it.

- You have full control over how it's used and maintained.

- You can customize or resell it later.

Cons:

- Huge upfront cost (new trucks run $120K+, used can be $40K–$90K).

- All repairs fall on you.

Buying might be right for you if:

- You have strong personal or business credit.

- You can put down at least 10–20%.

- You plan to grow your fleet and want long-term equity.

Real Talk: I didn't drive, but I did buy a semi-truck myself — because I saw the profit potential and wanted to run a trucking business, not just work in one. Ownership gives you leverage, even if you're hiring someone else to drive it.

Option 2: Renting Short-Term

Renting is great when you're:

- Testing the waters before committing.

- Covering a temporary need (like an extra route or driver).

- Saving up to buy later.

Downsides:

- You're paying for a truck you don't own.

- Mileage limits and restrictions apply.

Popular rental companies: Penske, Ryder, Enterprise Truck Rental.

Option 3: Leasing a Truck

There are two kinds of leases:

- Lease-to-own: You pay monthly with the option to buy at the end.

- True lease: You return the truck after a set time with no ownership.

Watch the fine print. Some lease deals have balloon payments, strict maintenance requirements, or limits on how you can use the truck.

CHAPTER 6

Insurance Ain't Optional

Insurance might not be glamorous, but it's non-negotiable. It's the difference between staying in business and going broke from one accident. And trust — it's one of the first things that separates serious carriers from broke hustlers.

What Insurance Do You Need?

Here's the bare minimum required by FMCSA:

- Primary liability: $750,000 (but most brokers require $1 million)

- Cargo insurance: $100,000 (to protect the freight you're hauling)

- Physical damage: Covers your truck itself if you own or lease it

- Non-trucking liability (NTL): Covers personal use when you're off dispatch

- Occupational accident/workers' comp: Especially if you have drivers

You'll need an insurance agent who understands commercial trucking — not your cousin's Allstate rep.

1099 vs W-2 Drivers: Let's Break It Down

This is where a lot of new owners mess up.

- 1099 drivers are independent contractors. You don't take taxes out, but you also don't control their schedule or provide benefits.

- W-2 drivers are employees. You're responsible for withholding taxes, unemployment insurance, and workers' comp.

If you treat someone like an employee but pay them as a contractor, you can get fined heavily.

If you outsource driver management to another company or dispatch service, make sure the agreement clearly states who is liable for taxes, insurance, and compliance.

How Much Will It Cost?

Premiums vary wildly based on:

- Age of your truck
- Where you're based
- Driving record of whoever's behind the wheel
- Whether your authority is brand new

Expect to pay $10K–$20K+ per year for one truck. New authorities usually pay on the higher end — but it does get better over time.

Can You Outsource All of This?

Yes. Some entrepreneurs choose to:

- Buy the truck

- Lease it to a carrier with active authority

- Let them manage insurance, compliance, and drivers

This hands-off approach can still be profitable, but you must have a clean contract. Make sure you understand how payment splits work, how risks are shared, and what happens if something goes wrong.

Booked & Branded Publishing

CHAPTER 7

Who's Going to Drive This Truck?

Hiring, Managing, and Building a Team That Moves the Mission

Let's keep it real — not every trucking business owner has plans to get behind the wheel. And guess what? That's perfectly fine.

Whether you hold a CDL or not, this chapter will walk you through one of the biggest decisions you'll face: how to staff your truck and structure your team — especially if you're building a business that doesn't require you to do the driving.

By now, you already understand the difference between CDL-required vs non-CDL setups (see Chapter 2), but this chapter will help you answer:

- "Who's driving?"

- "How do I hire them legally?"

- "Can I outsource operations and still be successful?"

Let's break it all the way down.

Option 1: Drive the Truck Yourself (Solo Owner-Operator)

If you hold a CDL and want to be hands-on in your business from the ground up, driving your own truck is a low-overhead option. You earn all the income directly, maintain full control, and gain firsthand experience.

Pros:

- Full earnings go to you
- Great learning experience
- Builds direct relationships with brokers and shippers

Cons:

- Physically demanding
- Business growth is capped by your time and energy
- You'll still need support for admin, dispatch, etc.

Boss Insight: Many women start this way to stack capital, then scale by hiring others. If you're new to the industry, this path can build confidence fast — but it's not the only way.

Option 2: Hire a Driver and Run the Business From the Top

This is where things get exciting — and strategic.

Just because you don't drive doesn't mean you're not in the driver's seat of the business. If you're reading this and thinking, "But I've never been behind the wheel of a semi," welcome to the club — I haven't either. Yet I still purchased my own truck and built a business around it.

What matters most is how you structure your team and legal responsibilities.

Two common staffing paths:

A. Hire as a W-2 Employee (Traditional Driver)

This means you treat the driver as your employee. You withhold taxes, offer pay on a schedule, and provide tools or benefits.

B. Hire as a 1099 Contractor (Independent Driver)

This means the driver is technically self-employed, but running your freight through your business.

Pros:

- Less paperwork and tax obligations
- Flexible structure for both parties

- Popular with experienced drivers who want independence

Cons:

- Less control over behavior, hours, and branding

- IRS penalties if you misclassify someone who should be an employee

- No built-in loyalty — they can walk away anytime

(For hiring third-party drivers under your authority — easy plug-and-play)

If you're not planning to drive your truck yourself, there are plenty of ways to find qualified drivers who can operate under your authority. You can post on sites like Indeed, CDL life, or Ten street, or work with recruiters who specialize in placing drivers. You can also connect with experienced drivers through local trucking schools, industry Facebook groups, or job boards like Truckers Report. Just make sure you vet them properly — check their CDL status, experience, and safety history before putting your asset in someone else's hands.

Strategy Note: The IRS has strict tests to determine if someone should be classified as a W-2 employee vs 1099. If you control the route, equipment, hours, or offer regular pay — you may need to classify as W-2. When in doubt, consult an employment attorney or payroll service.

Option 3: Lease Your Truck Under Someone Else's Authority

Let's say you're not ready to get your own MC number or take on full compliance yet. You can lease your truck — or your driver and truck — under an established carrier's authority.

Here's how it works:

- A larger carrier holds the authority
- You lease on your truck (and maybe your driver) to them
- They handle insurance, DOT compliance, and more
- You earn a percentage of every load

Pros:

- Fast entry into the industry without full compliance burden
- Access to freight and established load networks
- Reduced risk while you learn the ropes

Cons:

- You split earnings (typically 70/30 or 80/20)
- Less control over who your clients are
- Limited branding — you may have to run under their logo

Real Talk: This is a great option for women who want to start smart and safe — especially while learning the business or getting financial footing.

Option 4: Outsource Business Management to a Third-Party

Don't want to manage hiring, dispatch, compliance, and maintenance all by yourself? You can outsource those tasks to a fleet management company.

This is often used by investors, busy professionals, or absentee owners.

You still own the truck, but a management company handles:

You simply collect a percentage of the revenue, minus their management fee.

Pros:

- Hands-off management

- Experts run your fleet like a well-oiled machine

- Great for investors or passive owners

Cons:

- You'll pay a cut (often 10–25% of revenue)

- Less transparency unless you choose a trustworthy partner

Option 4: Outsource Business Management to a Third-Party

Quick Comparison Chart

Model	You Drive	Who Runs Operations	Income Control	Risk	Scaling Potential
Solo Owner-Operator	☑ Yes	You	100% yours	Moderate	Limited to your time
W-2 Driver	✘ No	You	High	Higher (payroll, insurance)	High
1099 Driver	✘ No	Shared	Medium	Medium (legal classification risk)	High
Leased Under Another Authority	✘ No	Other carrier	Shared (70–80%)	Low	Medium
Outsourced Fleet Management	✘ No	3rd party	Passive	Low	Very High

Final Thoughts: You're Still the Boss

No matter which model you choose — whether you're in the truck, behind a desk, or managing from a beach with WiFi — you are still the CEO.

Don't let anyone tell you you're not a real trucking business owner because you don't drive. You own the truck. You pay the insurance. You handle the decisions. That makes you the one in charge.

And with the right support system — from drivers to dispatch to compliance — you can build something massive without ever starting an engine.

Booked & Branded Publishing

CHAPTER 8

Money Moves: Setting Up Business Banking & Taxes

Your truck might run on diesel, but your business runs on cash flow. Let's get into the financial setup that keeps your company legit, funded, and tax-ready.

This chapter covers:

- Choosing the right bank
- Bookkeeping systems
- Business credit basics
- Taxes & write-offs

Step 1: Open a Business Bank Account

Once your LLC and EIN are approved, head to the bank and open:

- A business checking account
- A savings account (for taxes or reinvestment)

Recommended banks for trucking businesses:

- Navy Federal (if you're eligible)

- Chase or Bank of America (national access)

- Bluevine or Novo (online options with low fees)

Pro Tip: Keep your business and personal funds completely separate.

That's how you stay audit-proof and professional.

Step 2: Choose a Bookkeeping System

Use accounting software or apps to track:

- Fuel

- Repairs

- Tolls

- Meals

- Loads & revenue

- Insurance

- Driver pay

Good options:

- QuickBooks

- TruckingOffice

- Rigbooks

- Excel (for the DIY crowd)

Step 3: Build Business Credit

Yes, your trucking business can have its own credit score — and that credit can unlock trucks, fuel cards, and funding without using your SSN.

Start by:

- Opening Net 30 accounts (Uline, Grainger, Quill)

- Paying invoices on time

- Getting a D-U-N-S number from Dun & Bradstreet

- Applying for a fuel card or business credit card (after 60–90 days of activity)

Step 4: Understand Taxes

As a trucking business owner, you're responsible for:

- Quarterly taxes (federal and possibly state)

- Heavy Vehicle Use Tax (Form 2290) if your truck is over 55,000 lbs

- State franchise/business taxes depending on your location

- W-2s or 1099s if you hire help

Write-offs to track:

- Fuel

- Maintenance

- Cell phone

- GPS and ELD fees

- Lodging while on the road

- Per diem for meals

- Training and licensing fees

Hire a CPA or tax pro familiar with trucking. Trust me — they'll save you more than they charge.

CHAPTER 9

Paid: Invoicing, Factoring & Payment Terms

So you've booked the load and delivered it like a pro. Now let's talk about getting your money.

Option 1: Direct Pay from Brokers

Most brokers pay on Net-30 or Net-45 terms. That means you might not get paid for 30–45 days after delivery.

Pros:

- No middleman
- Full payout

Cons:

- Long wait
- Ties up your cash flow

Option 2: Use a Factoring Company

Factoring companies buy your invoices and pay you instantly, then collect from the broker later.

You'll get 85–95% upfront, and the rest (minus fees) once the broker pays.

Pros:

- Get paid within 24–48 hours
- No chasing brokers for payment
- Helps new carriers stay afloat

Cons:

- They take 2–5% as a fee
- Some lock you into contracts
- Not all brokers work with all factoring companies

Top factoring companies for new carriers:

- RTS Financial
- OTR Capital
- Apex Capital
- TAFS

Compare rates, contract terms, and customer service before choosing. A bad factor can hurt you more than help.

What Goes in an Invoice?

Your invoice should include:

- Your company name, address, MC#, and DOT#

- Broker or shipper details

- Load number and delivery date

- Agreed rate

- Rate confirmation sheet

- Proof of delivery (POD)

Send invoices promptly and keep digital copies of everything.

CEO Insight:

The quicker you get paid, the quicker you can reinvest — in fuel, maintenance, another load, or another truck.

Don't just focus on booking loads. Focus on how money moves in your business — and how to keep it flowing without stress.

CHAPTER 10

The 10 Commandments of Fleet Tracking

Powered by Real-World Strategy from the Inside

If you're going to run a profitable trucking company — whether it's just you in a box truck or a full fleet of semis — you need visibility, accountability, and control. That's where fleet tracking comes in. This isn't optional. It's how you protect your profits, your people, and your paperwork.

I'm not sharing this as a theory.

Through my experience working with companies as a fleet management advisor at Verizon Connect, I saw firsthand how the right GPS, ELD, dashcam, and fuel card systems made the difference between high-revenue efficiency and costly chaos. From one-truck operations to 100+ unit fleets, the success stories all had one thing in common: visibility.

These aren't just best practices — these are commandments for protecting your business from day one.

Commandment 1: Track Every Truck in Real Time

Real-time GPS tracking shows where every truck is, 24/7. Whether you're hauling Amazon freight, hotshot loads, or dedicated contracts, you need to know:

- Where your trucks are
- If they're moving or stopped
- Whether routes are optimized
- If drivers are meeting deadlines

Companies using fleet tracking save $200–$500 per truck, per month by eliminating:

- Inefficient routes
- Unauthorized stops or side gigs
- Theft
- Idle time that burns fuel

Recommended Tools: Verizon Connect, Samsara, Motive, Matrack

Commandment 2: Use Dashcams to Protect Your Fleet

Install dual-facing dashcams — one lens on the road, one on the cab. These protect you by recording:

- Accidents
- Traffic stops

- Delivery disputes

- Unsafe driver behavior

Dashcams are your silent witnesses. When insurance companies or DOT come knocking, footage could be the difference between a clean claim or a $20,000 headache.

Commandment 3: Use an ELD (Electronic Logging Device)

If your truck is over 10,001 pounds and operating across state lines, you'll need an FMCSA-compliant ELD to track driver hours. Most GPS systems now bundle ELDs and allow:

- Real-time log auditing

- HOS violation alerts

- Integration with dispatching

Don't risk being out of compliance — the fines stack up fast.

Commandment 4: Get a Fleet Fuel Card

Fuel is your #1 variable expense — and fleet fuel cards are how smart owners take control.

Why you need one:

- Save $0.10–$0.50 per gallon

- Limit purchases to fuel only

- Track who bought what, where, and when

- Flag fraud and prevent cash misuse
- Separate business from personal use
- Some cards help build business credit

Expert Insight:

I've seen carriers save over $1,000/month on fuel with smart fleet card usage alone. And when I owned my truck, switching from debit to a fuel card stopped unnecessary driver expenses instantly. Sometimes the upgrade isn't about what you gain — it's what you stop losing.

Top Picks: Motive Fuel Card, WEX, Fleet One EDGE, Fuelman

Commandment 5: Track Maintenance Like a CFO

Breakdowns happen — but they don't have to ruin your week or your profit margin.

- Preventive maintenance schedules

- Oil changes and tire rotations

- DOT inspections

- Brake and transmission servicing

Use tools like Fleetio, a simple spreadsheet, or even Google Calendar to stay organized. Missing maintenance deadlines is the fastest path to expensive surprises.

Commandment 6: Monitor Driver Behavior

This is your name, your DOT number, and your insurance premium on the line.

Watch for:

- Speeding

- Harsh braking

- Long idle times

- Out-of-route behavior

You can use your tracking system to coach good drivers and eliminate high-risk ones before they cost you thousands.

Commandment 7: Store Records Digitally

Use Dropbox, Google Drive, or a trucking CRM to organize:

- Rate cons

- PODs

- Maintenance receipts

- Driver records

- Insurance policies

- Fuel reports

If DOT audits you or a claim is filed, you need everything ready — instantly.

Commandment 8: Know Your Numbers

What's your:

- Cost per mile?

- Empty miles ratio?

- Average gross revenue per truck?

- Fuel spend per load?

- Net profit after dispatch/factoring?

Most small fleet owners have no clue — and that's why they never scale. Data isn't optional; it's your edge.

Commandment 9: Be Proactive, Not Reactive

Waiting until a tire blows or a driver quits to solve a problem is a losing strategy. Weekly fleet reviews — even if you only have one truck — will keep your business tight:

- Check fuel and repair expenses

- Analyze broker performance

- Look at driver behavior reports

- Review ELD and maintenance alerts

If DOT audits you or a claim is filed, you need everything ready — instantly.

Commandment 10: Treat Tracking as a Profit Tool — Not an Expense

I've said it before and I'll say it again.
Fleet tracking pays for itself.

With the right system in place, you'll:

- Lower insurance costs

- Reduce idle time and fuel waste

- Prevent loss and fraud

- Streamline dispatching and reporting

This is the tech backbone of your business. Don't skip it. This is how you run a company, not just a truck.

Booked & Branded Publishing

CHAPTER 11

Dispatching, Load Boards, and Brokers

The Money is in the Movement

You've got your truck, your authority (or someone else's), your tracking systems, and your insurance squared away. Now what?

Now it's time to start making money — by moving freight.

This chapter breaks down the three main ways to book loads, how to keep control over your operations, and when to outsource vs. DIY.

The 3 Primary Ways to Book Loads

- Load Boards

- Dispatchers

- Direct Broker or Shipper Relationships

Let's break down each.

Option 1: Load Boards (DIY Hustle)

Load boards are platforms where brokers post available freight and carriers "bid" or claim the loads. Think of it like Uber for trucks.

Popular Load Boards:

- DAT One (Most respected, especially for semis)
- TruckStop.com
- 123LoadBoard
- Amazon Relay (Box trucks and cargo vans – more below)

Pros:

- Fast access to loads
- Great for new MCs
- Good for learning the market

Cons:

- Highly competitive
- Race-to-the-bottom pricing
- Time-consuming if you're the driver too

Pro Tip: Set alerts on your favorite lanes so you're not scrambling. And always check a broker's credit score and days-to-pay before accepting a load.

Spotlight: Amazon Relay

Amazon Relay is Amazon's own load board platform. It's designed for carriers to haul Amazon freight directly — often between their fulfillment centers or local delivery hubs.

It's especially popular with:

- Box trucks and dry vans
- New authorities looking to get started quickly
- Carriers that want consistent, shorter-distance freight

To qualify, you'll need:

- An active MC or DOT number
- Minimum insurance coverage (Amazon will specify the amounts)
- A reliable ELD
- Safety scores in good standing

Once approved, you can log into the Amazon Relay portal or app and book loads instantly — no phone calls or bidding wars.

Pros:

- Easy to get started
- Quick Pay available
- Transparent pricing

Booked & Branded Publishing

- Great way to stay loaded while you build broker relationships

Cons:

- Rates can be lower than market average

- Limited lanes depending on your location

- Strict on-time performance requirements

Pro Tip: If you're just starting out and struggling to book loads on traditional boards, Relay can help you stay moving while you build your rep

Option 2: Hiring a Dispatcher

A dispatcher finds loads for you, handles paperwork (rate cons, BOLs), negotiates rates, and communicates with brokers.

Typical Cost:

- 5%–10% of your gross weekly revenue

Great for:

- Drivers who don't want to deal with calls

- Busy owners with multiple trucks

- People who value convenience over control

Red Flags:

- Dispatchers asking for full MC login

- No written contract or service agreement

- Charging flat rates without guaranteeing loads

- Double brokering (illegal and shady)

Always check references and start with a trial week before locking into any agreement.

Option 3: Direct Broker or Shipper Relationships

This is where real profit and consistency start to show up.

Once your MC gets more established (90+ days, solid delivery history), brokers and shippers start to trust you.

Benefits:

- Higher-paying freight

- Consistent lanes

- Faster payments (Quick Pay or net-7)

- Less competition

How to Build Relationships:

- Deliver loads on time and communicate well

- Ask brokers about recurring lanes

- Use your factoring company's broker search tool

- Follow up and stay professional

This is how you shift from "surviving" on load boards to building a real trucking brand.

Managing Dispatch In-House (If You Want Control)

Some owners prefer to keep dispatch in-house from day one.

If you:

- Love numbers

- Can negotiate with confidence

- Want to learn the business inside and out

...then managing your own dispatch might be the move — at least in the beginning.

Must-Haves:

- A laptop or tablet

- Load board subscriptions

- A clear dispatch process

- Time during the day to monitor loads and broker emails

Other Load Booking Models

- Co-Drivers or Partnered Carriers: Some teams split dispatching duties between owners

- Freight Agents: Licensed intermediaries who connect you with brokers (sometimes commission-based)

- Dispatch Services for Owner-Ops Only: Some dispatchers work exclusively with owner-operators and offer add-on services like invoicing and compliance

Before You Accept Any Load...

Run this checklist:

- Is the rate per mile acceptable for the lane and equipment?
- Is there deadhead involved? (Miles run with no freight)
- Is the broker reliable? (Look them up!)
- What are the pickup/drop windows?
- Is lumper or detention pay included?
- Do I need extra insurance for this freight type?

You don't just want to move freight — you want to move smart.

Don't say yes out of desperation — low-paying freight will bleed your business dry faster than you think.

Final Thought

Whether you dispatch yourself, hire a team, or build broker relationships — always track your average gross, net, and rate per mile.

This is where profitability lives.

Booked & Branded Publishing

CHAPTER 12

Scaling SMART–From One Truck to a Fleet

Don't Just Drive — Build Something

Let's be real — not everybody gets into trucking to build a fleet.

Some people are perfectly happy running one truck, staying hands-on, and keeping their business lean. And there's nothing wrong with that.

But if you're reading this book, I have a feeling you're not here just to drive.

You're here to build. To grow. To scale.

This chapter is your playbook for turning a single-truck operation into a profitable, sustainable fleet.

When Is It Time to Add a Second Truck?

Adding a truck is a big move — and timing matters. Here's when to seriously consider expansion:

- You're consistently profitable for 3–6 months
- You've built strong broker or shipper relationships

- Your systems (insurance, dispatch, compliance) are tight

- You have cash or financing in place for another unit

- You're mentally ready to stop driving and start managing

Real Talk: Don't scale chaos. Fix your first truck's business model before duplicating it.

Crunch the Numbers — First, Always

Before you start truck shopping, know your margins:

- What does it cost you to run one truck each week?

- What's your net after fuel, maintenance, insurance, and factoring?

- Will a second truck double your profit — or double your stress?

Make sure your first truck is cash flowing enough to either:

- Pay for your lifestyle while the second gets up to speed, or

- Contribute to buying that second truck outright

Owner-Op vs. Company Driver vs. Lease-On

Here are your options for staffing your growing fleet:

They bring their own truck and run under your authority. You take a percentage (commonly 15%–25%) in exchange for:

- Dispatching

- Compliance

- Insurance

- Fuel card and factoring access

Pros: Low capital investment, strong partnerships
Cons: Less control, requires solid onboarding systems

Company Driver (You Own the Truck)

You buy the truck, hire a W2 or 1099 driver, and manage the entire operation.
Pros: Full control, brand consistency
Cons: More liability, more payroll stress

Lease-on to Another Carrier

If you don't want to build an authority yet, you can scale quietly by adding trucks and leasing them onto another MC — just like someone would with you.

This is often overlooked but powerful when used strategically.

Systems to Have in Place Before You Scale

- Fuel Cards and ELDs that scale with your team

- Fleet Tracking Tools like Verizon Connect or Samsara

- Onboarding Documents (driver files, contracts, DOT forms)

- Load Tracking SOPs

- Weekly Reporting on revenue, mileage, rate per mile, fuel usage

- Maintenance Schedules and service records

Scaling is really just systemizing.

If you can't hand someone a clipboard and a checklist, you're not ready to duplicate yet.

Funding Options to Scale

- Business credit lines (Navy Federal, Divvy, Bluevine)
- Equipment financing or truck loans (Ally, Mission Financial, CAG)
- Investor partnerships (use sparingly — always protect ownership)
- Revenue-based funding (based on weekly income trends)

Avoid using personal credit unless you're backed by strong savings or other income. Keep trucking growth tied to business capital when possible.

CHAPTER 13

From Hustle to Legacy

A Real Talk Reflection for Every Woman Building
Something Bigger

From Hustle to Legacy: Why You Can't Stop Here

Let's pause for a second.

You didn't just pick up this book to play around with an idea. You picked it up because something inside you — maybe a whisper, maybe a scream — said, "I want more." And that "more" isn't just about money. It's about freedom. Ownership. Legacy.

That's the difference between a hustle and a business. A hustle gets you through the week. A business changes your trajectory. But a legacy? That shifts everything for you and the generation after you.

Trucking can be all three. But only if you build it that way.

Hustle is the Start — Not the Finish Line

Hustling isn't bad. In fact, most of us had no choice but to start there. You figure things out on the fly. You wear all the hats. You get it done because there's no safety net.

where hustle meets strategy

But what happens when you burn out? When your driver quits? When your truck needs $8,000 in repairs and your backup plan is... a prayer?

That's when hustle hits its limit.

The goal isn't just to move loads. It's to move with a plan.

Think Like a CEO — Not Just a Carrier

You're not just running a truck. You're running a business. And if you want to win in this space long term, you've got to start thinking like the CEO you are:

- How will I structure my company so I can scale?

- What assets am I building that will keep generating income if I step away?

- Who do I need on my team so I'm not doing this alone forever?

- How will I protect my time, my credit, my health — and still grow?

If you're always in survival mode, you'll never see the big picture. You've got to step out of the day-to-day grind long enough to build something with structure and longevity.

This Is Bigger Than You

Let's be real — most industries weren't built with women like us in mind. Especially not trucking. But we're here now. And we're not just taking a seat at the table — we're bringing our own damn table, chairs, and blueprint.

Booked & Branded Publishing

When you build your business right, you become a model for someone else:

- Your daughter sees a boss, not a burnout.

- Your niece sees options, not just jobs.

- Your friends stop doubting and start doing.

Your courage makes space for someone else's confidence. That's how legacy works.

Real Talk From the Inside

When I worked with companies through Verizon Connect, I saw what separated the businesses that grew from the ones that failed. It wasn't always about the number of trucks. Sometimes the biggest fleets were the messiest.

The winners had:

- Systems

- Data

- Discipline

- And a mindset that said, "This is bigger than a load board. This is my empire."

And that's what I want for you.

Build What Doesn't Exist Yet

If no one in your family ever owned a business — you get to be the first.

where hustle meets strategy

If no one around you understands why you're doing this — do it anyway.

If you're scared? Build through the fear.

This industry doesn't need more drivers. It needs more visionaries. More women who aren't afraid to learn the business side, delegate with purpose, and walk into rooms like they belong — because they do.

What Legacy Looks Like (It's Not Always What You Think)

Legacy isn't just what you leave behind. It's what you live right now:

- Building credit in your business name.

- Protecting your assets with insurance and compliance.

- Documenting SOPs so your kids or employees could step in.

- Buying equipment in your business's name.

- Creating job opportunities for others.

- Showing up every day with integrity.

This is the stuff they won't show you on Instagram. But it's what lasts.

Let Your Truck Fund the Bigger Vision

What do you really want this business to do for you?

- Buy land?

- Pay off debt?

- Fund your skincare line or real estate portfolio?

- Give you the freedom to be present for your family?

Don't lose sight of that. The truck is a tool. The load is the vehicle. The vision is yours.

You don't have to stay behind the wheel forever. But you do have to drive the direction.

Final Words From Your Ghostwriter Turned Guide

You already have what it takes. You've got the drive, the mindset, and now — the playbook.

So promise yourself this:

- Don't stop at hustle. Don't stop at one truck. Don't stop at survival.

- Build it solid. Build it smart. Build it so strong they can't knock it down.

- Your empire on wheels is real. And this is only the beginning.

The Real Win: From Hustle to Business

When your trucking business becomes:

- Something you can step away from

- A brand that people recognize

• A system that runs without daily scrambling

...that's when you've shifted from driver to owner to CEO.

Scaling doesn't just mean more trucks.

It means more structure, more consistency, and more opportunity.

Whether you stop at 3 trucks or build a 20-truck empire — do it smart, and do it solid.

You don't have to drive forever.
You just have to drive the vision — and
build something that lasts.

Booked & Branded Publishing

CHAPTER 14

Dear Reader, One Year From Now...

An open letter from Stephanie Williams, MBA — Strategic Business Consultant, Author, and Builder of Beauty, Brains, and Business

Dear Reader,

If you're reading this letter one year after finishing the book... pause for a second and really take that in.

You did it.

You made it through the hard parts — the doubt, the late nights, the second-guessing, the moments where quitting looked easier than continuing. You pushed past the overwhelm and stayed in the game long enough to become the version of you that used to just be a dream.

I don't know exactly what your life looks like right now — maybe you're running a truck with a team, maybe you're in the thick of building your dispatch company, or maybe you've expanded and now you're mentoring other women. But I do know one thing for sure:

where hustle meets strategy

You didn't just read a book. You took action.

A Year Ago, You Were Unsure

You may have picked this book up thinking, "I don't know where to start. I don't have all the answers." And guess what? You didn't need to.

You just needed the courage to start — and you had that all along.

Remember when everything felt complicated? When things like MC numbers, load boards, DOT compliance, or fleet tracking sounded like a foreign language?

Now it's your native tongue.

You've learned the business. You've faced the fire. You've owned your title — not just as a driver or a dispatcher or an admin behind the scenes — but as a CEO.

You Are What Legacy Looks Like

One year later, you've probably already changed the trajectory of your family.

Maybe you:

- Took your first vacation in years — and didn't worry about money

- Showed your kids that a woman can run a logistics company from her laptop

- Bought your second truck and named it after your grandmother

Booked & Branded Publishing

- Walked into a funding meeting with your LLC, EIN, and fleet data ready to go

Whatever your version is — you are walking proof that legacy isn't reserved for tech bros or corporate giants.

It's built by everyday women with a vision and a willingness to move.

If You Needed a Reminder Today...

Let this letter be it.

You didn't come this far just to survive. You came this far to own your path, your story, and your outcomes.

I hope this year stretched you. I hope it humbled you in the right ways and empowered you in the most unexpected ones.

I hope you stopped asking for permission.

One More Thing...

If you ever find yourself back at a crossroads, wondering whether you're qualified, whether you're too late, or whether this road is still for you — come back to these pages.

Come back to this letter.

You already proved it to yourself once. You can do it again. And again. And again.

There's still more empire to build.

So here's to Year 2.

More growth. More freedom. More strategy. More power moves made in silence.

Keep glowing. Keep building. Keep driving your vision.
I'm rooting for you — always.
With respect, love, and relentless belief in your greatness,

Stephanie Williams, MBA
Strategic Business Consultant, Author, and Builder of
Beauty, Brains, and Business

Booked & Branded Publishing
www.bookedandbrandedpublishing.com

CHAPTER 15

The CEO Quote Wall + Power Prompts for Trucking Bosses

For the days you need inspiration — and the days you need direction.

Part 1:

The CEO Quote Wall

A curated collection of quotes to keep your mindset sharp and your mission alive.

You don't just have to be in trucking.

You can run this thing like a business — and you can run it like a boss.

"You don't have to see the whole staircase.
Just take the first step."
— Dr. Martin Luther King Jr.

---

*"If they don't give you a seat at the table,
bring a folding chair."
— Shirley Chisholm*

*"You can't build a legacy off hustle alone.
You need systems, structure, and strategy."
— Stephanie Williams*

*"Faith it until you make it. Then scale it
with confidence."
— Stephanie Williams*

*"Don't play small because no one in your
circle is thinking big." — Unknown*

*"Legacy isn't about what you leave behind.
It's what you're building right now." —
Stephanie Williams*

Booked & Branded Publishing

"Don't wait to be picked. Be the boss that cuts the check." — Myleik Teele

"You are your ancestors' wildest logistics department." — Anonymous (but it sounds like you!)

"If you knew how many people were watching you silently win, you'd never consider quitting." — Unknown

"I didn't come this far to play with potential." — Stephanie Williams

Part 2:

Power Prompts for Trucking CEOs

Use these questions to reflect, journal, and realign with your vision — at every stage of your journey.

where hustle meets strategy

1. What does ownership mean to me — beyond money?

What kind of decisions will I get to make differently when I'm no longer depending on someone else's paycheck?

2. Why did I choose trucking — and what will I use it to fund?

Is this the end goal, or is it the vehicle to something bigger?

3. What limiting beliefs about business, leadership, or money do I need to unlearn?

Who taught me those things — and are they still serving me?

4. What does my trucking business need from me right now: more hustle, or more systems?

What's one system I can set up this week that will make my life easier next month?

5. How will I know when I've built a real business — not just a busy job?

What does freedom actually look like to me?

6. What part of my business makes me feel most powerful?

Is it making deals? Mentoring others? Running the numbers? How can I lean into that more?

Booked & Branded Publishing

7. Who do I need to become to lead this business into its next level?

What habits, decisions, or boundaries does that version of me have?

8. Am I building a business that can run without me?

If not, what's one thing I can delegate, automate, or systemize this month?

9. What story will my kids, nieces, or younger sisters tell about what I built?

What example am I setting — and how can I make it even stronger?

10. If I trusted myself 100%, what would I do differently today?

Would I take the leap? Raise my prices? Add a truck? Walk away from something that no longer aligns?

Final Thought

Your trucking business is more than a side hustle or survival plan. It's the beginning of a blueprint. A model. A movement.

Use these quotes and prompts as fuel — because the real empire isn't just built under your name...

It's built under your leadership.

CONCLUSION

The Road Is Yours

You made it through the trucking Bible — and now you've got the blueprint.

This journey won't always be easy. You'll hit potholes, detours, and breakdowns (literal and figurative). But if you stay focused, stay legal, and stay hungry — you can build something powerful, something profitable, and something that lasts.

Whether you're driving the truck yourself or managing a fleet from your laptop, always remember:

You don't just have to be in trucking.

You can run this thing like a business — and you can run it like a boss.

See you at the top.

GLOSSARY

- Authority (MC Number): Your permission slip from the FMCSA to operate as a for-hire carrier.

- Bill of Lading (BOL): A legal document detailing what's being shipped, where it's going, and who's responsible.

- Broker: The middleman between shippers and carriers.

- CDL (Commercial Driver's License): A special license required to operate certain types of commercial vehicles.

- DOT Number: Identification number issued by the Department of Transportation.

- ELD (Electronic Logging Device): Device that tracks a truck's driving hours to ensure HOS compliance.

- Factoring: Selling your invoices to a third party for quick cash.

- FMCSA: Federal Motor Carrier Safety Administration — the regulatory body over commercial trucking.

- Load Board: Online marketplace where carriers can find available freight to haul.

- Rate Per Mile (RPM): What you earn per mile driven — a key metric for profitability.

REFERENCES

- FMCSA: www.fmcsa.dot.gov

- DOT Compliance Guide: www.transportation.gov

- Amazon Relay Requirements: relay.amazon.com

- DAT Load Board: www.dat.com

- Trucking Authority Setup:
  www.fmcsa.dot.gov/registration

- Fuel Card Programs: RTS Financial, Comdata, EFS

- Fleet Management Tools: Verizon Connect, Motive,
  Samsara

- Insurance Carriers: Progressive Commercial, OOIDA,
  CoverWallet

- Equipment Financing: CAG Truck Capital, Mission
  Financial, Balboa Capital

- ELD Providers: KeepTruckin, Geotab, Garmin

WORK WITH ME

Want a book like this for your business or personal brand?

What I Offer

As a Strategic Business Consultant and elite ghostwriter, I help entrepreneurs, educators, and CEOs turn their expertise into high-impact books, courses, and premium digital products — fast.

Whether you want to:

- Establish credibility in your industry

- Attract high-ticket clients

- Launch a trucking course or coaching program

- Or simply create something powerful and passive...

I'll help you do it — professionally and profitably.

Want this exact book setup?

I create full book + workbook packages for clients — just like this one.

Be sure to download the free workbook using the QR code or link included — it's packed with tools, checklists, and templates to help you implement everything inside.

Ready to build your own empire?

www.bookedandbrandedpublishing.com
hello@bookedandbrandedpublishing.com

Scan for printable tracker & digital copy

ABOUT THE AUTHOR

Stephanie Williams, MBA, is a powerhouse Strategic Business Consultant, real estate investor, and founder of Booked and Branded Publishing — a boutique agency helping entrepreneurs turn their knowledge into profitable books, brands, and businesses.

With a career that spans corporate B2B sales, real estate investing, digital product creation, and small business consulting, Stephanie brings a rare blend of street-smart hustle and boardroom-level strategy.

She's worked with startups and national companies alike, including Verizon Connect, where she specialized in fleet tracking solutions for small to mid-sized trucking companies — giving her unique insight into the operational challenges new owners face.

Stephanie has purchased and managed multiple properties across Georgia, flipped homes, launched high-converting digital offers, and coached women through business mindset shifts and systems.

She also runs a nonprofit initiative focused on economic empowerment and access for underserved communities.

She wrote this book to help everyday women build generational wealth in the trucking space — no fluff, no gatekeeping. Just real talk, real strategy, and a belief that your vision deserves to roll.

Booked & Branded Publishing